A GUIDE FOR SUCCESSFUL BUSINESS

WITH

INFLUENCER MARKETING

Table of Contents

INTRODUCTION

Influencer Marketing is a modern marketing strategy where the emphasis is mainly on individuals rather than the whole target market. Such people, known as influencers, have a profound effect on the marketing activities of many other potential brand consumers. Over the last ten years, the proliferation of social media has dramatically revolutionized interaction and has a substantial impact on the world of business.

Influencer Marketing is now one of the most powerful tools in the toolkits of a marketing team. It is not expected that this effective strategy will soon disappear with most of the major brands. Research shows that it will probably continue over the years. Why? People don't trust the brands anymore. These traditional marketing methods no longer influence many people, and now they are influenced by people they believe and respect.

On the other hand, many brands still misunderstand "influencer marketing," making it a useful tool. To tell the truth, 74% of purchases are made using word of mouth, and influencer marketing are one of the most efficient ways of driving word-of-mouth sales. No wonder marketers are increasingly adopting influential branding and marketing strategies to achieve their business goals and goals. This segment outlines the most common marketing failures of influencers in order to be successful and reduce underestimated costs.

CHAPTER ONE

The incredible rise of social media

It is very important to have in mind some statistics in order to understand the enormous and endless power of social media.

Facebook, the largest social media platform in the world, has 2.4 billion users. Other social media platforms including Youtube and Whatsapp also have more than one billion users each.

These numbers are huge – there are 7.7 billion people in the world, with at least 3.5 billion of us online. This means social media platforms are used by one-in-three people in the world, and more than two-thirds of all internet users.

Social media has changed the world. The vast and rapid adoption of these technologies is changing how we choose partners, how we access information from the news, and how we organize to demand political change.

When did the rise of social media start and what are the largest sites today? Who uses social media? Here we answer these and other key questions to understand social media use around the world.

We begin with an outline of key trends and conclude with a perspective on the rate of adoption of social media relative to other modern communication technologies.

Social media started in the early 2000s, the first social media site to reach a million monthly active users was MySpace – milestone achieved around 2004. This is arguably the beginning of social media as we know it.

In the chart below we plot monthly active users, by platform, since 2004.

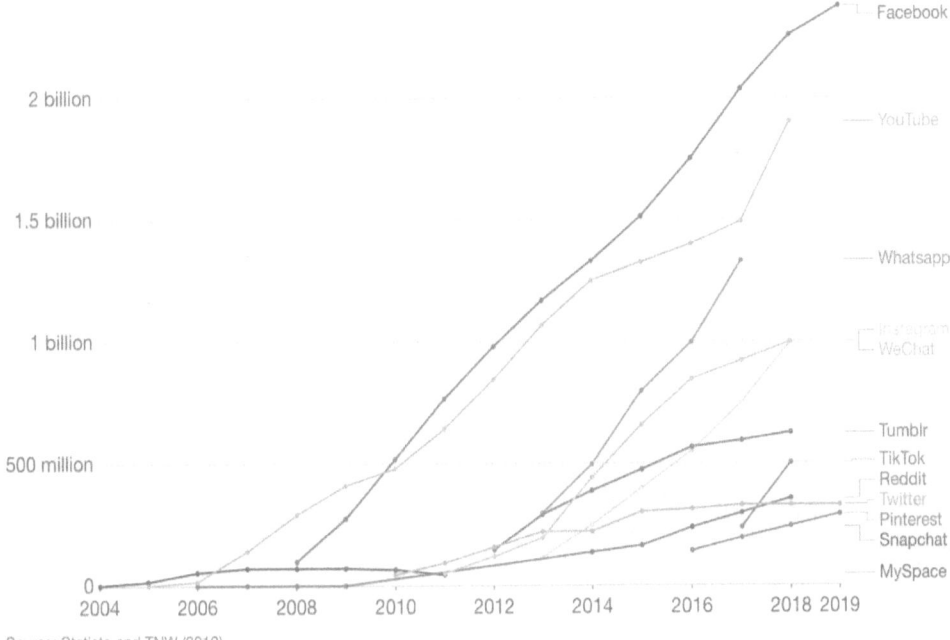

Number of people using social media platforms

Estimates correspond to monthly active users (MAUs). Facebook, for example, measures MAUs as users that have logged in during the past 30 days. See source for more details.

Facebook

2 billion

YouTube

1.5 billion

Whatsapp

1 billion

Instagram
WeChat

Tumblr
TikTok
Reddit
Twitter
Pinterest
Snapchat

500 million

MySpace

0
2004   2006   2008   2010   2012   2014   2016   2018 2019

Source: Statista and TNW (2019)

This chart shows that there are some large social media sites that have been around for ten or more years, such as Facebook, YouTube and Reddit; but other large sites are much newer.

TikTok, for example, launched in September 2016 and by mid-2018 it had already reached half a billion users. To put this in perspective: TikTok gained on average about 20 million new users per month over this period.

The data also shows rapid changes in the opposite direction. Once-dominant platforms have disappeared. In 2008, Hi5, MySpace and Friendster were close competitors to Facebook, yet by 2012 they had virtually no share of the market. The case of MySpace is remarkable considering that in 2006 it temporarily surpassed Google as the most visited website in the US.

Most of the social media platforms that survived the last decade have shifted significantly in what they offer users. For example, Twitter, didn't allow users to upload videos or images in the beginning. Since 2011 this is possible and today more than 50% of the content viewed on Twitter includes images and videos.

With 2.3 billion users, Facebook is the most popular social media platform today. YouTube, Instagram and WeChat follow, with more than a billion users. Tumblr and TikTok come next, with over half a billion users.

Some social media sites are particularly popular among specific population groups. The aggregate numbers mask a great deal of heterogeneity across platforms – some social media sites are much more popular than others among specific population groups.

In general, young people are more likely to use social media than older people. But some platforms are much more popular among younger people. This is shown in the chart where we plot the breakdown of social media use by age groups in the US.

For Snapchat and Instagram, the 'age gradient' is extremely steep – the popularity of these platforms drops much faster with age. The majority of people under 25 use Snapchat (73%), while only 3% of people over 65 use it.

Since these platforms are relatively new, it's hard to know how much of this age gradient is the result of a "cohort effect". In other words: it's unclear whether today's young people will continue using Snapchat as they become older. If they do, the age gradient would narrow.

Use of social media platforms by age group in the US

The share of adults in the United States who say they ever use the following online platforms or social media apps in 2019. This is shown by age group.

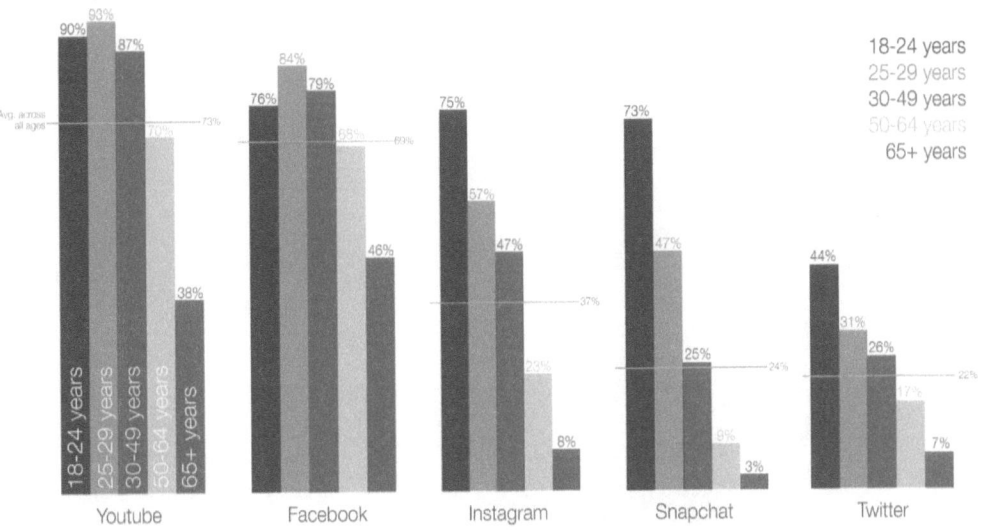

18-24 years
25-29 years
30-49 years
50-64 years
65+ years

Data source: Pew Research Center (2019).

Let's now look at gender differences.

In this other chart we show the percentage of men and women who use different platforms in the US. The diagonal line marks parity; so, sites above the diagonal line are those more popular among men and sites below are those more popular among women. (Bubble sizes are proportional to the total number of users of each platform.) For some platforms the gender differences are very large. The share of women who use Pinterest is more than twice as high as the share of men using this platform. For Reddit it is the other way around, the share of men is almost twice as high.

Percent of men and women using social media platforms in the US, 2019

Estimates correspond to US adults who say they ever use these online platforms or apps. Bubble sizes are proportional to the total number of users of each platform.

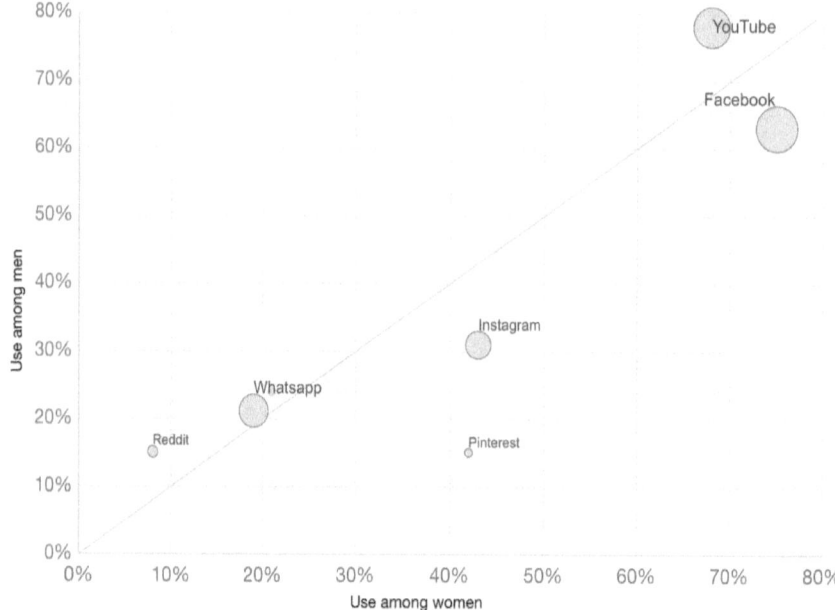

Source: Pew Research Center (2019), Users by social media platform (Statista and TNW (2019))

In rich countries almost all young people use social media.

From a back-of-the-envelope calculation we know that, if Facebook has 2.3 billion users, then at least 30% of the world uses social media. This is of course just an average – for some world regions, and specifically for some population groups, usage rates are much higher.

Young people tend to use social media more frequently. In fact, in rich countries, where access to the internet is nearly universal, the vast majority of young adults use it.

The chart here shows the proportion of people aged 16 to 24 who use social networks across a selection of countries. As we can see, the average for the OECD (Organization for Economic Co-operation and Development) is close to 90%.

If today's young adults continue using social media throughout their life, then it's likely that social media will continue growing rapidly as internet adoption expands throughout lower-income countries.

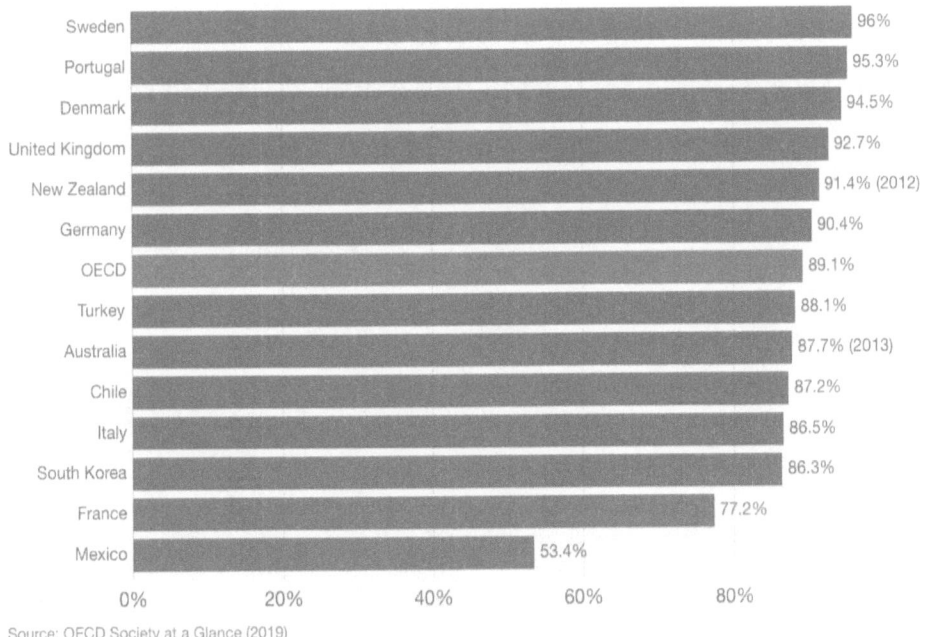

Percentage of young people engaging in social networking online, 2014

Percentage of young people, aged 16-24, engaging in social networking online. The OECD average is unweighted. Data refer to 2014 or closest available estimate.

Source: OECD Society at a Glance (2019)

The rise of social media in rich countries has come together with an increase in the amount of time spent online.

The increase in social media use over the last decade has, of course, come together with a large increase in the amount of time that people spend online.

In the US, adults spend more than 6 hours per day on digital media (apps and websites accessed through mobile phones, tablets, computers and other connected devices such as game consoles). As the chart shows, this growth has been driven almost entirely by additional time spent on smartphones and tablets.

According to a survey from the Pew Research Center, adults aged 18 to 29 in the US are more likely to get news indirectly via social media than directly from print newspapers or news sites; and they also report being online 'almost constantly'.

There is evidence that in other rich countries people also spend many hours per day online. The next chart shows the number of hours young people spend on the internet across a selection of rich countries. As we can see, the average for the OECD is more than 4 hours per day, and in some countries the average is above 6 hours per day.

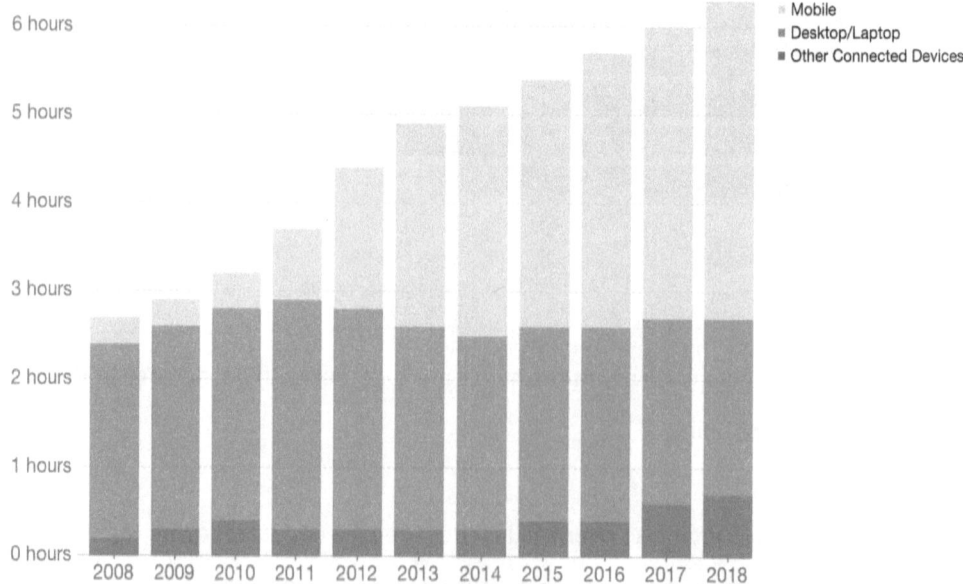

Daily hours spent with digital media, United States

Average hours per day spent engaging with digital media (e.g. digital images and videos, web pages, social media apps, etc.) The data for 'other connected devices' includes game consoles. Mobile includes smartphones & tablets. All data includes both home & work usage for people 18+.

- Mobile
- Desktop/Laptop
- Other Connected Devices

Source: BOND Internet Trends (2019)

Daily time spent on the internet by young people, 2016

Hours per day spent on the internet by people aged 14-24

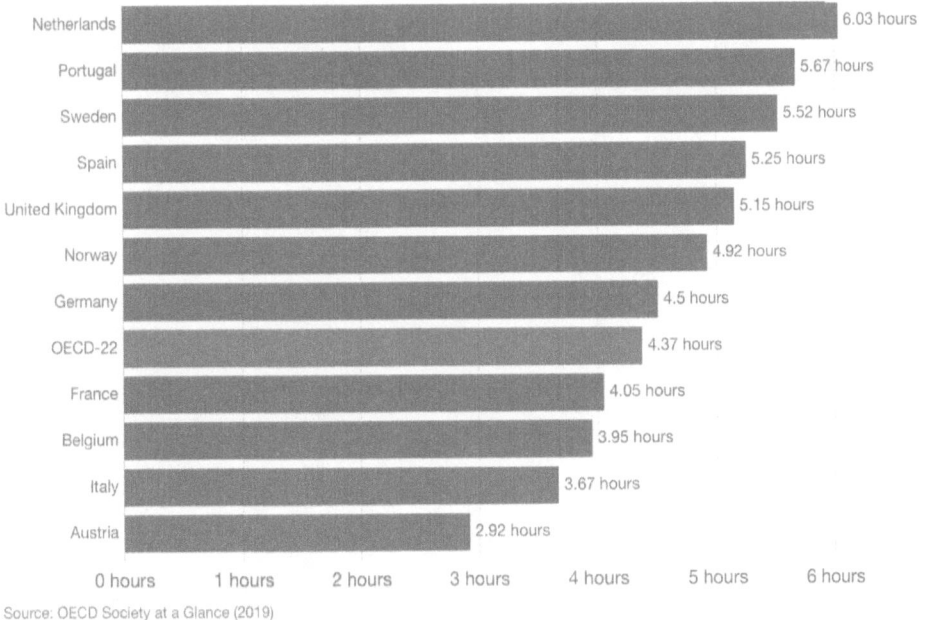

Source: OECD Society at a Glance (2019)

Let see some perspective on how fast and profound these rapid changes are.

The percentage of US adults who use social media increased from 5% in 2005 to 79% in 2019. Even on a global stage the speed of diffusion is striking: Facebook surged from covering around 1.5% of the world population in 2008, to around 30% in 2018.

How does this compare to the diffusion of other communication technologies that make part of our everyday life today?

The following chart provides some perspective.

Social media's growth in the US is comparable – in speed and to some extent also in reach – to that of most modern communication-enabling technologies, including computers, smartphones and the internet.

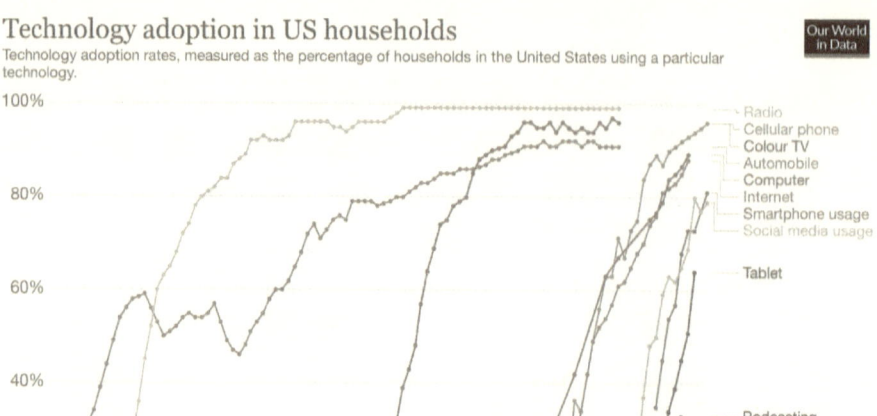

The rise of social media is an extraordinary example of how quickly and drastically social behaviors can change: Something that is today part of the everyday life of one-third of the world population, was unthinkable less than a generation ago.

Influencer Marketing Platforms

A lot of marketers around the world are looking for ways to connect more effectively with their audiences. It is becoming very clear that most consumers have confidence in their customers rather than in brands. In other words, consumers have great and real strengths, so Brands need to change their marketing strategies to create a better experience for their users.

We all know that the idea of influencer marketing is a slow but consistent one. Contrary to traditional marketing, most companies and brands are prepared or must invest time to develop genuine and authentic relationships with their influencers. Result is measured throughout the new brand loyalist acquisition and weighed don't often by cents and dollars, but Achievement without additional funds is difficult to achieve. So, if your marketing strategy is excellent, you need to invest time and money, either you get more trust and money.

The actual marketing takes time and attention, you do not need to focus on tasks like campaign management and influence relationships but simply look at them. The most important tasks are to find the right people for your work, to monitor campaigns, to measure your success or failure, but remember that failure motivates you to work and to improve your success. You do not have to do these multiple tasks most of your time, because there is different platforms that can do this for you. If you save time in accounting tools that will allow you to focus on how to increase your earnings, these platforms reduce the time-sweeping administrative tasks that distract you from achieving your goals.

Such apps can be a preliminary move for you to gain your popularity as an influencer slowly and also ease your tasks as you get going, thus helping you create solid campaigns without hurting your head.

In September 2015, TapInfluence launched TapFusion the first automation software and had Volvo, Target, Lego, and The Gap as its first clients. An impressive list that serves as proof of the effectiveness the automation applications. The software itself is more like an influencer, and Brands and Agencies can search the massive influencer database of the software. They will work with them to determine what the campaign will look like when it is launched. Once campaigns are launched, the software collects all relevant data to feed the analytics and reporting engine to social media users worldwide. TapFusion is an incredibly efficient working platform, but it's not a small agency or company platform. Register for a demo, and an automated email will appear in your email saying that you will require $25,000 a quarter to invest in customer solutions. If it sounds too big for you, that's not yours. However, if your budget meets that demand, your $25,000 will be spent very well.

Speakr, it's less of a software platform, more of an agency that combines brands with influencers. But it doesn't mean that technology isn't a second thought, that every time you work on your clients, the software is there, it is the driver how it represents its influencers. Its network surpasses 20,000 social media stars, people who have not only a great success but also consistent commitment to a loyal audience. The audience is part of the requirement to be ambassadors in one of the Speaker's influencers. Speakr offers brands the chance to connect and develop content at a time with many people. The potential Speaker is not involved. Speakr has listed several big companies and brands such as Verizon, Toyota, BMW, Honda, Disney, Microsoft, and Universal Studios, and they are just a few with Speakr's performance.

Traackr. There would be no influential marketing platform without a profound analytical engine and a wide network of influencers. Traackr's platform focuses on the management of influencer relationships since few companies recognize influencer marketing by trust. It focuses primarily on the success of the brand with its long-term impact. Traackr lists brands with influencers and their audiences that promote familiarity and build authenticity and confidence. HP, Forbes, EMC, Intel, and Travelocity are only a few of the big companies which have been expanding their reach with Traackr.

Revfluence. This platform is called a' self-service platform' and has access to 150,000 users in these enormous social network's platforms. It is good for agencies and brands that create their own marketing campaigns at home. The Creator Collaboration Toolkit (CCT) is a strong focus on the actual content creation, streamlines the process of working with influencers, supports built-in tools in the creation and management of each content, tracks the progress and reach of each campaign and ensures engagement with the audience. This platform contains Quest Nutrition, Birchbox,

Dermalogica, and Scopely on the brand list they have, they may not have household names, but they can be taken up to the next level.

NeoReach. A tiny company, looks like they are trying to define themselves fully. In addition to their offer to manage "Managed Campaigns", they design and run the entire campaign on behalf of their customers, and customers will only jump into their dashboard to see the situation of their campaigns.

Social book. A new platform that could help people gain insight. It is the world's first real-time analytical engine to influence performance and a great platform that can help most influencers monitor their performance. This operates by entering the username and/or channel URL of the influencer, and then the social book engine begins to run and produce statistics, then the influencer will receive the account file. Simple as 1, 2, 3!

Influencer Marketing: Deep Understanding and Its Basics

We know that It's all a buzz, any move a celebration makes is a big gossip in the Celebrity Industry. Well, there are also many effective methods in and marketing, which we call a "hot problem", and "influencer marketing" is what has grown up and stands out among them.

Today we live in a world full of business and marketing. When you think about making an ad? What's up to you? Headlines of the magazine? Television Commercials? I'll tell you the truth; perhaps they aren't as effective as before. Time changes, successful coverage changes too. Now, influencers just talk some magic phrases about their 1-3-minute video, and then Voila! Sales come true! Those who influence them large and large supporters, can distinguish you from the chaotic and old-fashioned methods of advertising, but they are also of massive value to your brand in the end.

So, what is marketing influencer? This segment addresses nearly all your questions about advertising influencers.

Before we dig deep into her knowledge and insight, first, let's define two words: the ability to have an effect on someone's behavior, development, character and decisions, and even the effect itself.

Marketing is a business activity that promotes or sells products and services.

Therefore, when the two terms overlap, influencer marketing is a kind of advertising that uses "influencers" to persuade others to purchase what is advertised or sold.

There are two forms of marketing influence: social media marketing: refers to the series of activities aimed at gaining traffic and attention via social media sites.

Content Marketing: means a type of marketing involving the creation, production, and distribution of online materials such as videos, blogs, and publications in social media. It does not promote a brand in order to generate interest in its products and services.

Both have different definitions, but it appears that they are related.

Influencer marketing may be a hot problem right now, but it isn't fresh, in fact, influence marketing has been alive since social media websites were discovered. Celebrities, Leaders and sports enthusiasts are the first influencers and would partner with them in their specific fields in support of products and services. Here are some good features Influencer Marketing has been armed with: Unique social media communication gives everyone the chance to express their own perception. Anyone who talks and has an internet connection is invited to share its content. Anyone who owns a smartphone can produce high-quality imagery with their personal social media account and share it with the world. And who among them has the biggest and most fascinating commitment will increase and become an influencer.

Authentic Indeed, influencer marketing is real; you read it correctly. Have you seen an online commercial about how to remove bad fats in your belly? Have you ever felt a single cell in your body believing in those ads? Or did you see a TV advertisement about a soap that could whiten your skin immediately after just one wash? How is that possible? No offense, but why and why does influencer marketing is more authentic and more effective than traditional advertising that you see through online, TV ads, etc.? Why influencer campaigns are more organic and genuine than traditional advertising? First of all, influencers were noticeable, and the product or service provided are used by them. They are seen as role models and leaders that are examined. Investing the time, effort, and money to fertilize and interact with your audience is much worthwhile because these influencers are more trustworthy and have become the most reliable customer outlets. In other words, people listen to it and believe in it.

Influencers allow you to drive traffic to your website with your brand image. It can create a stronger connection between you and your clients, improve your SEO, and attract media coverage. An influencer is your Superman when you need a hand to boost the name of your brand and generate a big buzz on different social media sites. They will help you to target the right audiences, grow your social media network, share ideas about content creation, and improve your SEO.

Cost-effective Marketing Influencer

If you are tired of posting flyers anywhere in your region already but have no sales at the end of the day. The best method for you is influencer marketing. Although the cost for influencer marketing is not set, whether you offer them free products, pay them performance-based, or others recommend a "flat rate" value. However, that influencer marketing has the best ROI. Several investigations have already shown that it is more affordable and effective than traditional advertising.

CHAPTER TWO

Strategies Most Marketers Misunderstood in Influencer Marketing

Influencer marketing is one of the most effective tools in the toolkits of a marketing team today. The majority of the brands that use this effective strategy are not expected to disappear in the near future. Research shows that it is likely to continue over the years. Why? People don't trust the labels anymore. Many people are no longer influenced by traditional marketing methods and are now influenced by the people they trust and respect. On the other hand, numerous brands still do not understand what "influencer marketing" is, making it an effective tool. In reality, 74 percent of purchases are made with word of mouth, and influencer marketing is one of the most effective ways of driving word-of-mouth sales. It is no wonder that marketers increasingly adopt influencer branding and marketing strategies to achieve the goals and objectives of their companies.

The segment outlines the most common marketing failures for influencers to be obvious in order to succeed and to avoid underestimated costs.

Uncomprehending the audience

Your audience is your critic; they will be your customers if they want your product. If you don't know your audience/client, you can't never develop a long-term and effective marketing strategy for influencers. A marketer who has not yet developed a genuine marketing personality is advised to stop their programs until they know who their customers are and what their interests are in order to achieve and interact with the brand. In order to establish a marketing person, it should be noted that marketers need to understand purchasing practices, demographic information, pinpoints, and psychographic information, and conventionally, all these statistics can be collected through client reviews.

Your marketing would not work if you did not work with the right influencer in your campaign with influencer marketing. Influencer marketing across all channels, niches, and target audiences is not equally effective. It is very recommended that you collaborate with YouTube influencers if you endorse a beauty product since it is very successful in videos than a simple picture of your product and a post on Facebook, Instagram, or Twitter.

Short-term outcomes

If you have just started advertising through an influencer, you cannot expect a good outcome in a single snap. In some cases, overnight marketing campaigns could produce results for a powerful influencer. But influencer marketing will take time to take effect, particularly for brand names and enterprises that do not use e-commerce. Confidence and patience are recommended. It should be remembered that successful promotions through impact lead to brand awareness. When a candidate knows your brand, he or she still has to take a marketing funnel process, consideration, and decision-making steps before making a purchase. Sure, it takes time for the results to be obtained.

Adopting to use analytics is one of the most precise ways to be updated and to determine whether your marketing influencer is efficient or ineffective. You need to monitor and measure the results of your campaign on all types of platforms, so you can find out which portion of your marketing campaign needs to be improved. You will find several online platforms to help you evaluate your feedback and success in your campaign.

If you fail to convey expectations to your influencers, it is important to formulate your expectations when you work with influencers clearly. You should provide your influencers with a rundown of your campaign's goals and objectives. Collecting and including your collected marketing staff will help your influencer to succeed. You may also want to include analytical information you find valuable for the target audience when marketing.

Focusing on the wrong KPI's (Key Performance Indicator) Marketing influencers is a powerful marketing method, but all in the world have its own limits. Marketers must ensure that influencer marketing is the right way to go. It is recommended that you concentrate on KPIs that match your brand, product, and activity, not simply focus on sales, but start being genuine! Generally, an influential Marketing campaign to influence KPIs in connection with low-funnel behavior.

Avoid that strategy because it "once" failed. Just because you once failed to do so does not mean that you should give up. Marketers do not avoid advertising simply because one of their marketing campaigns has not been successful. Instead of quitting, use this failure to improve your marketing if you have failed. You have to understand why the campaign failed so that the next time you set out a marketing campaign, you can implement better strategies and ideas. Please remember, failures are one of the challenges you face when entering marketing for influencers and learn from them is the key to success.

Before launching your campaign, make sure you consider this question: Where should my audience click to act when engaging with my I.M. (Instant messaging)? Content?

If you plan to use I.M. to drive traffic on your website, make sure you create a website that will allow your visitors to use the next step. It is important to ensure that the designed web page is checked if it works perfectly on both mobile and P.C.s. Associate the action call with an I.M. campaign, and ensuring it's optimized for your goal is key to I.M.'s success.

To choose an ineffective agency to handle influencer partnership advertising will have a big negative impact. A lot of marketing agencies provide I.M. utilities and services, but guess what? Not everyone of them has valuable experience. I mean, strategies have a little, but not a deep understanding. Therefore, your marketing cannot succeed. Select an agency with experience working with influencer marketing strategies that appeal to your business.

This will direct you towards your achievement.

Influencer Marketing Is Now Bigger Than Digital Ads

Everywhere you look, people look at their phones online and interact with various social platforms.

If you haven't heard that, we're all pieces of influencer marketing.

We continuously inhale and exhale advertising influencers every day, and many of us don't fully realize what they are. As the world modernizes, people's voice expands, we have entered a new era of digital marketing, a more organic form of marketing carried out by influencers.

The content of influencers can be framed as testimonial advertisements when they either play the role of a potential purchaser or are third parties.

This recognizes the individuals who affect potential buyers and orients advertising efforts around them.

"Advertising with influencers turns influential people into client supporters." Before we get into more specifics about this form of advertising, you should know clearly what it is.

This method of advertising focuses on the message of the product to a customer rather than large groups of customers.

The person is called "the influencer", who is paid to speak out for your company.

These influencers may be the potential buyers themselves in this influencer marketing game. In general, they play the role of content writers, journalists, bloggers, CEOs, creatives, advertisers, or consultants.

We are linked to others around them and are asked for guidance and opinions and considered to be influential.

The two main ways of power marketing are content marketing and social media marketing.

How does marketing influence?

Nowadays, users react more to social media ratings or a person's opinions than they believe in advertising.

This is the foundation for advertising influencers where influencer blogs about the goods through his personal and social media.

People tend to believe what the influencers have to say in the press about something.

Several marketing companies had no influence on their radars as it is such a unique product method. In many cases, it is out of their control because more of an individual voice than a standard static company ad takes hold. The same interactive and emotional response by the consumer is not given to digital ads.

The social media feedback and ratings on a brand or product add to the product or brand showcased and form the new product placement platform.

Why is marketing influencer now larger than digital advertising? And how did this occur?

Confidence and honesty are very important marketing factor.

We all know which media we trust and distrust and, in most cases, simply by the header of the subject.

Traditional media is riddled with disinformation, and the general customer would rather interact socially with its products or services.

Consumers cannot purchase goods or services unless they are fully assured that the product or service is in every way suitable for their needs.

If you influence the mind, you are believed to have the world in your hands, and that is what influencers do.

Influencers have established relationships to build trust. Much commitment and encouragement have been made to build these links.

When it comes to building relationships and creating a positive message around a particular brand, influencer marketing is higher than digital advertising.

Let's shed some light on the influencer marketing as "THE NEXT BIG THING".

As the world has moved into social media, customers are looking at other consumers to tell their purchasing decisions.

They are now looking to each other and to their favorite characters, which are consolidating huge follow-up on YouTube, Instagram, Snapchat, Pinterest, LinkedIn, Twitter, Facebook and other platforms, instead of looking at companies, as they have done before.

The increase in the influence of social media has created a world of possibilities; it has opened the flood of new waterworks for brands to connect directly and to a larger degree with consumers by means of more organic natural marketing methods like new word of mouth.

It offers an online messaging system for a better description. With each social media interaction or reaction, it enables hundreds of more people to view your message via their social networks.

While digital ads contain precise information about the goods, an influence on the market has its own ways of attributing people to a more interactive consumer arena that has an organic life to the message with all of the exact descriptions and information about products and services.

The influencers are depending on updated information about their products or services, and the message can also be posted over many days or weeks.

It is considered an influencer's job to collect and send the message to consumers all the things about the marketing campaign.

The influencers are often paid for their work in order to ensure this. If not paid, the company they work for or in some cases share content with their readers will give them incentives only to educate and to encourage interaction between the network.

In comparison to digital ads, influencers often "do not sell something" and simply share information to create a more productive impact network or to encourage participation and discussion on issues that can truly help. You may choose to adopt other marketing strategies such as an e-mail newsletter to advertise advertising services or products.

The static digital ad does not provide context as it includes poster and banners ads and has no opinions-oriented target.

Old and outdated information could soon turn consumers away.

People are more likely than advertisements to trust others. Marketing influencers have the concept of the "word of mouth", which sums up how people trust influencers. Where ads can be nothing more than stories or exaggerations for many consumers, people will probably trust their friends and society when they say about a certain product.

Influencers shape ties with the market; influencer campaigns are very useful in this process. The trust gained allows the market to flourish; after all, advertising depends on consumer confidence so that the consumer engages with the advertisement.

The marketing of influencers is much easier and simpler than digital marketing.

Not only is the way to attract people easier, but the way to do so does not take much effort other than the creative element.

In this period, in which everything is simplified through the Internet, effective advertising by the social platforms and digital facilities was made possible.

You start writing about this and post about it online, and thousands of viewers visit your blogs and journals within minutes.

The online facility helps connect people all over the world.

"Everything should be made as simple as possible, but not simpler."
Albert Einstein

Advertising with influencers have the advantage of performing digital wonders, allowing people from around the world to communicate.

All questions about an item are answered instantly and are often much more welcomed than e-mail, ticket service, or any other form of Q&A distribution.

Whether it is social media or content-oriented market, people will immediately receive answers to many of their questions concerning a product in influencer marketing and view the comments that make the viewership rather exceptional.

When advertising on social media, where advertisements are put in all the commonly visited social sites, people are made aware of other views on goods, which allow them to analyze their purchasing decisions.

In addition, they are connected with other people on social media (that act as influencers in this case) who tell you about many goods and therefore solve many questions.

In the case of the market-driven content, influencers are already available to answer any questions from the customers. This removes any doubts about a product.

It's powerful. But it is easy.

Influencer markets are themselves powerful. The quality of influencers share is strong and real. We have the ability to gain respect and trust, all that is important.

Thoughts and opinions are shared by influencing markets, and even with consumers who live miles away, better relations are established.

The writings can wonder all those bloggers, reporters, content writers, and CEOs who depict the market accurately through their writings and depend on the evidence, opinions, and ideas of many consumers. The marketing roots with any social platform are pretty strong and not easy to cut down.

These writings are far more convincing than digital ads consisting of a few photos and slogans. The writings speak of the feedback and views of other people and influencers, a quality that is surely lagging on the digital ad market. We could have just seen the peak of the digital advertising and ad market.

When social media are filled with videos about the products, the benefits of digital ads usually made up of banners and posters have become much less significant.

Living objects are more attractive automatically than life. Influencers have started to use video content to influence the people who prove to be another advantage of influencer marketing.

Famous people as influencers

Consumers are greatly influenced when their favorite celebrities tweet about a particular product.

This has become an increasing area of influence marketing that celebrities are used to attract people to a specific product. Like television advertisements in which celebrities are used to influence social media, they are used today to post on how a particular product are made.

This practice requires no convincing practice, as many people blindly believe in the quality of the thing when it is bought by their favorite celebrity.

Online feedback

When the market is influenced by social media, consumer feedback becomes very important for marketing purposes. The market is growing with positive feedback and similarly decreases if the feedback is not in favor of goods and services.

People today greatly believe in consumer ratings and online opinions.

This concept of online ratings and participation is largely driven by influencer marketing and thus is rapidly growing.

Honest consumers opinions are more valuable than ads for opinions and ideas.

In the world of influencer marketing, people's opinions are just as important influencers on social sites.

If not all, most of people's feedback and opinions on a given service or product are honest.

In the case of digital advertising, there is hardly any shared opinion as such communication is not feasible on the ad platform.

The time-efficient promotion of influencers is immediate and is dependent on the established relationship between the influencer and their network.

The idea that influencer advertising takes over digital ads can only happen now.

In some other years, influencer marketing has been estimated to take over all other marketing strategies and become the largest marketing practice by 2022.

Influencer Marketing and its myths

You might wonder exactly what marketing influences are. Okay, advertising is based on individuals rather than on particular brand. Influencers are very influential and have enormous effects both in the United States and around the world. Marketing influencers can be considered highly custom marketing.

Over the last few years, influencer marketing is much more popular and prevalent in today's business climate. Many of the people who support this approach want to do it and get results, while others don't do it well and don't get the results they hope to achieve. The reality is that influencers have gained knowledge and experience in their specific niche. It is not, however, safe to assume that every advice given by each influencer is necessarily perfect advice for all.

If any of the influencers you follow say your reasoning doesn't (or can't) happen, you should listen to your gut. It probably won't end in the way you are told by the influencer. Given this, it is important for you to bear in mind that there is a lot of false and/or useless information and to find out what information is valuable and which information should be disregarded because it will not be of any benefit to you.

If a person is popular, then it follows that he or she is an influencer. It's good that a person is popular, but it's never necessarily associated with his being an influencer. It takes time and a lot of hard work to achieve influencer status. A person can be popular, on the other hand, because of charm and charisma. That has nothing to do with the knowledge or experience of that person. As always, choosing quality over quantity is much more important. In this country, with so much pressure and knowledge coming from so many viewpoints, it is important that you can separate valuable information from useless information. In fact, it is critical to your business ' success.

Influencers won't agree to work with you unless you pay: neither is this necessary. Obviously, any businessman is in business to make money eventually. No one wants to do it free of charge. This doesn't assume, however, that every time money is the engine. It really depends on what you offer and what the influence a person wants to get out of the relationship with you and your business. Not everyone wants their opinion to be paid for. Trading is quite popular in the business world. The chances are very good that the influencer finds something valuable and that you can make a deal with him or her very well.

It is nearly impossible to build partnerships between brands and influencers: If you start something new or attach leverage to your content marketing plan, you need to realize that you can always do this. It is important for you to understand, however, that every relation takes place and that the relationship with your influence is no different. You have to evolve and maintain the relationship. You'll probably start to see results after a short time. The more effort you make, the better it will be.

The return on investment (ROI) ends your link to the influencer: you can't go beyond the facts. In fact, that is only the start of the relationship. You should set your goals at the very start of the relationship (that is, decide what you expect from the relationship) and work towards those goals with the influencer to accomplish them. What you really want is a lasting relationship with the impact guy. This influencer (and any other influencers you connect to) should help you to get your company to the next level, which is what you want.

Does influencers' marketing cancel other established forms of marketing?

This is by no means true. Influencer marketing is like incoming and outgoing marketing more effective if it works in conjunction with other marketing types. You want to get the most from your marketing efforts, and to do this, you need to have a deep understanding of the different kinds of advertising and the types of results you can expect for your company. Promotional influencers will theoretically take a broad range of activities, and many people are delighted to engage in receiving your marketing efforts.

Marketing influencer is definitely a marketing approach that you should consider for your company. You should, however, bear in mind that it works best in combination with other advertising forms that also perform well for your company and produce positive results. Marketing influencers should not instill fear. If so, the solution learns so that you can understand how useful it can be for your company. The core of influencer marketing is, of course, trust, and we all understand that strong relationships are based on trust.

CHAPTER THREE

The Influence of Psychology in Marketing

Once it relates to marketing success, you can't go anywhere unless you have a relationship with the other person and build a sense of trust, reputation, and a belief over time that you are the expert on your subject. There's no way to go without the friendship. Here it is important to understand that psychology plays an important role in your success.

The relationship behind everything

When you first meet a person (in a professional context), emotionally / humanly, you begin to connect. With a lot of effort and some luck, you're going to share a mutually and satisfying beneficial relationship with another person. These and the other attributes listed here before are the building-up of a strong and significant relationship. Obviously, until you can really connect with anyone in any meaningful way, you need to understand the way the person believes and a keen sense of the needs and wishes of that person. You have to wrap your mind around the person so that you have a chance of a meaningful relationship. This is when psychology comes beyond (and into) the conversation. If you do not understand (at least to some degree) how the other person thinks, you will not succeed.

If you think of your own marketing strategy, you'll begin to realize that you would probably struggle to do anything without the psychological aspect. The reality is that you are in a world where you compete hard, and if you are the one person chooses by others, you will have to solve whatever problem the other person has. This goes far beyond solving a problem. You need to consider how the other person feels and what he or she can do based on these feelings. When you look at two companies that provide the same goods and/or services, what makes the consumer prefer one company over the other has nothing to do with what is actually delivered. What makes the person choose depends on how you feel (or the other owner of the business). That's your margin. To be successful, you need a clear understanding of what influences the other person to make certain decisions.

What determines the person is in a both those paths: Successful marketing is a very simple concept, in fact. In order to get with the other person from point A to point B, you must persuade him or her that he or she will be better off if he or she chooses you over anyone else. All right, you realize at this stage that there's emotion behind any decision a person makes. Interestingly because they are not all exactly the same human beings, they do not all come to a decision simultaneously or have to make the same effort to reach a decision. Most people make decisions quickly and easily (these decisions are sometimes the right ones and sometimes the wrong ones too). Other people are working on the decisions they face. A third person has almost unlikely decision-making ability and does his best to avoid being put in that role.

What do you do when you have a hard time deciding? The truth is that sometimes it will be hard to make a decision. If you are in this difficulty, it may be helpful that you pay attention to and go along with what other people will do in your situation. You will, of course, ensure that you do not lose yourself. It can really make your decision much less intimidating if you emulate what other people decide. When you see that it's not so difficult to make a decision, the next time you decide, you won't shy away. The more choices you can make, the easier it will be for you. Just remember to think before you make your decisions. The last thing you want to do is to have regrets that can affect every aspect of your business.

Don't always do what is easier: the easy decision sometimes isn't the right choice for your company. Sometimes it turns out you don't have to rely on your decision. If you feel it takes a lot of effort to make decisions, then what? Nothing bad ever came from hard work. And for you, it's good practice. Instead of being afraid to make decisions, you have to try to make informed, educated decisions. It helps you grow as an entrepreneur and a person. One thing you should always keep in mind is that whatever decisions you take, you should first study so that you have a good sense of the outcomes. You will still be better informed than if you do not do your housework, even if not every last detail can be predicted.

What are you doing if you have too many choices? There are situations in which you face several different choices, and you don't know where to go. That may be awesome for you. You might not feel so intimidated if you approach it in a simplistic way. It can help you to list the advantages and disadvantages of each scenario. After that, it will be easier to make your decision, and it will become obvious to you in which direction. Sometimes the best condition is that you are making only one decision so that your choice is clear. Life does not always work that way, however. You just have to make the best of what you can and do.

Don't be influenced by the wrong things: Sometimes you have a highly appealing decision that resonates with you. Unfortunately, your business may not always be the right decision. Slowing down, weighing pros and cons is still a good idea, and then making an informed decision. One question you should ask yourself is whether you would be better off after the decision you are considering.

Psychology plays an important role in influencing decisions and thus helping you succeed. As a business owner, you can make a deep understanding of the other person through psychology (human behavior) as one of your drivers. Your marketing materials should reflect the human quality we all share. If you can wrap your mind about how the other person believes, you can get a grip on what they want and need.

Becoming an Influencer in Your Industry

How are influencers so vital to your company? Well, there are many different reasons how influencers are professionally important to you. Influencers bring credibility that only they can bring (beyond the reputation that you have demonstrated for your business).

At this point, you start wondering exactly what you are doing to become an influencer. Well, you can follow certain definitive steps to get there. At this point, however, it's important for you to realize that it won't be overnight. It will take you some time and effort to be the influencer you want to be.

Use the idea of influencer: an influencer is a person who has a lot of credibility, a person that has a very positive effect on your niche and your brand subsequently. Influencers also come with followers (a kind of entourage). Followers may come in different ways, for example, people who consistently follow blogs posted by the influencer or who frequently communicate with the influencer. Influencers can come in different forms and sizes at the same time. The one thing everyone has in common is that all influencers are able to influence other people. In other words, they are very powerful people, and they should not be rejected. There are influencers, and their word carries weight. You can consider them figures of authority. They are the gold standard on which your market strategy should be based. In fact, you are not the only person who knows the value of influencers. Other people also understand and take advantage of their value.

Focus on your niche: if you begin to take steps to become an influencer, first you have to decide exactly where you want your influence to live. This decision is based on where your passions lie. If you choose to be an influencer in an area you don't really touch, you can't pull it out. If you could not convince yourself of your commitment and your passion, exactly how do you expect others to be convinced of your passion and commitment. It's so simple. Nonetheless, it is important that you are closely connected to your niche so other people can also identify you with this niche. This is indeed an important part of your marketing. You want to be clear about other things. You only want to be linked to your niche. Otherwise, your status as an influential person will be diluted, and you won't be considered an expert.

Give people the opportunity of your understanding: in fact, it's another thing to be concerned (even to be a niche expert), but it's another thing altogether (and much more a gift) that you can tell someone else what you know, so that the other person can develop professionally because of this. Whether you can achieve this or not is a real test of your influencer status. The best way to do it (with all the online interactions that you have for your business) is to share content (in which form(s) you choose to share). Another great way to share your knowledge is through online discussions that are relevant to and compelling to others. It is also possible to post newsletters videos, blogs, and others. Keep in mind that you always pay close attention to your social media profiles. You don't want to be static for them. You have to update constantly your status in your social media profiles and keep people close to you in your social circles so that you can improve your friendship with them.

Tell other people your opinion: everybody loves knowing that their opinions and feelings are important. This is even more critical for you and your company as an influencer. Nothing like a silent influencer exists. In terms of this, it is a contradiction. The more people you meet, the more they know who you are and what you do. Both are key to your ongoing success. It's not as if you were trying to twist anyone's arm to get them to interact with you. They are ready participants as long as they are interested in interactions. You only have to make sure it's always the case. As an influencer, you can do this quickly. Even if you're not yet an influencer but are on your way to being one, this strategy will benefit you.

Network: networking has always been an integral part of the business process and will always be. You can network in person and online in both ways. It does not have to be one or the other, of course. You can also connect in both directions. You can only determine which approach works best for your company. The relationships themselves are at the heart of networking success. The truth is that not all people will take the time to attend network activities so that you have to be adequately versatile to make them work with others. When you network regularly with people, they will know you and start to trust you and consider yourself trustworthy, and whenever they need what you are offering, they will be at the forefront.

Realize the essentials of engagement: it is so important for you to reach your target audience. You will be halted in your tracks without involvement. You have the strength, however, to avoid this. Whether you are an influenced or an influencer, with everything you have to offer, others will want to hang around you and reap the beauty of what you had to offer.

Influencers in the professional world are extremely important and, and it's worth the time and effort to be an influencer. People will respect what you have to say and turn to you for the answers they don't feel qualified to give. Ensure that your interactions with influencers are part of your social media marketing strategy. It should be one of the building blocks of the base of your company. You will have a prominent role in your social networks, and your business will benefit from your hard work. In a world where it is more difficult than ever to draw the attention of other people, your reputation as an influencer would attract those people and keep them with you.

How to Start Influencer Marketing Campaigns That Work

Operating with influencers becomes the rule quickly. The days have ended even though it was easy to put your product on social media and expect good content and social media practice results. Many advertisers now believe that influencer marketing is a necessary measure as well as an effective strategy. The challenges of promoting your company are increasingly urgent. A multi-faceted approach is therefore needed in winning audiences.

Even for seasoned marketers, influencer outreach is a challenge. Some companies use one way or another to compensate influencers in order to gain favors. It's good. In reality, it helps to reward them, such as gratuities or discounts. Nonetheless, something must be more persuasive than these perceived incentives. Otherwise, you can just lose them with better offers to other companies.

Cooperation is one step in influencer marketing. It occurs after you have become your influencers friend, as you win their trust. Influencer-marketing examples, which we have had in the past, are the result of building an attractive content and establishing a relationship with those key persons in your niche.

Forget about hitting influencer. If you are at the heart of your business, your targets should be product development, content generation, and management of social media. We emphasize the importance of working on things you can capitalize on in the near future so that you have more opportunities to win influencers.

Social media is basically the most convenient marketing platform for influencers. This is where we are looking for the right candidates. That's where we're dealing with them. Collaboration with influencers usually takes place on social channels such as Instagram, Twitter, YouTube, and Facebook.

Influencers post from time to time. When they do it, they benefit from people and websites. Influencers are direct supporters to institutions too which they refer. This makes them the drivers and movers of social media.

Social media references may be in any form of content— text posts, pictures, or videos. There are also various ways to list you. An influencer can directly tag you. She/he can also mention you in a recent post. She/he can mention your brand, as well.

Start relationships

Making social media popular people shout a natural outcome of a good marketing strategy for influential people. It's easier to get people to consider you when you appeal to them. In other words, with your possible influencers, you must make friends and gain their trust.

Influencers with less than 10 K followers usually work with this. These people are more willing to work with people, especially those with significant track records, with brands in their niche.

In return, it's often a difficult task to make friends with people. Sometimes they're only relentless or too busy. Some celebrities in social media are cynical of followers who suddenly say favors to them and ask for them. If you can't make friends with them, give them something nice. It's up to you what you can sell. For a single mention, it can be a consumer review. It can be a free-month subscription to a continuous social networking service.

BLOG FEATURE

Nothing flatters brands more than an authority in their niche. You have this professional guy who has 100,000 followers on Twitter. He blogs about renovating kitchens and performs DIY demos. Every day, thousands of people read his blog because it's very informative and helpful.

You are offering options for cleaning sinks here. You want this man to show your material. Perhaps he could use your company to do a kitchen sink cleaning demo so that he can guide his viewers to try your brand himself. It is not so difficult to comprehend the rationale of someone discussing your company or writing a blog about it. Bloggers have been paid by companies for so long to feature their brand. Only now did we call this advertising influencer. Well, it's a form of it basically.

Your business is the focus of a blog post or story. This usually takes the form of a summary of testimony, which, I hope, does not sound too careful-otherwise people would be intrigued. Bloggers may simultaneously review or feature a number of products. You may ask them to include your product if this happens. This is one of their trust examples of influencing marketing we know are not too cumbersome.

Offer an acceptable bid

Influencers who manage blogs are busy animals. They are not your regular social media celebrities who simply blink in with a liner, selfies and memes. Bloggers conduct research at any moment, interview other people, work on a plan, or write their next post. You usually do not check your email to find out if someone is requesting a blog post. So, if you want to be heard, you can't refuse a bid. Again, this tactic works if you don't sound like a tedious, hopeless guy.

You can't ask any influencer to review your brand. The wrong influencer will not generate income and will only drain your money. The contents are important to your campaign and his/her audience is probably also your audience. If your brand isn't important to its content, influencers will decline your bid, how can a fashion blogger be expected to talk about camera accessories?

Considers make an outstanding bid. It's not easy to write a segment about your company. Nobody does it free of charge. Compensation is a key aspect of advertising influencers.

Be reasonable and realistic with your goals. It takes a while for material to be published. Don't make unreasonable demands, like requesting a short-term review. It wouldn't mind an influencer turning you down.

Within their niche, bloggers won't write anything.

Make your work easier. Consult on a blog post instead of giving them the whole job. Guest post, perhaps?

Provide pictures or videos, if needed. You're not hiring a writer, remember. You work with an influencer.

CHAPTER FOUR

Influencer Marketing Strategies for the Social Business

Influencer marketing is indeed a clever marketing technology. The emphasis is mainly on individuals rather than the whole target market. Such people, known as influencers, have a profound impact on the marketing efforts of many other potential buyers of a product. The social media explosion in the past ten years have innovated communication exceptionally and has a similar effect on the world of business. This has led to the development of several potential influencers who, because of business experience, are often very involved in social media (with many followers).

The concept of influencer marketing is not just about increasing awareness but rather about a positive impact on sales. The selection of a productive influencer is, therefore, highly sensitive to brands. Many customers today do not respond well to posters, newsletters, digital advertising, advertising, and other traditional marketing schemes. Costumers prefer to hear about independent brand research from a trusted individual. As a result, the use of marketing influencers becomes one of the most successful ways of attracting customers for all enterprises, including social enterprises (social benefits, social projects, non-profits, etc.).

Non-profit advertising and other public organizations require that the interests of their sponsors and clients they represent meet. Each social organization requires successful advertising regardless of its source of funding so that it can consistently meet the needs of donors and consumers while gaining positive value in return.

In this modern age of business, fundraising, non-profit advice, and profit-making advisory services uncover and reveal key development technology, including influencer marketing strategies. Influencer marketing techniques are constantly evolving. However, aligning itself with the right influencer opens the sales door for its loyal audiences and networks, giving them the chance to relate continuously to these audiences.

An important factor in the creation

An effective advertising influencer program is the identification and involvement of the most capable and best contextual influence on the brand. Social entrepreneurs could still improve the value successfully donor's eyes and satisfy the customers they serve by effectively using these features to target influencers ideally:

1. Public and reach: It is advantageous to target potential influencers with enormous follow-up on various social media platforms.

2. Relevant connections: This emphasizes the importance of targeting people with posts, comments, and messages with a degree of cohesion and keywords of the brand.

3. Quality and confidence: quality and trusted followers of influencers give potential customers greater capacity. This is measured by the special attention given to members of the audience who interact with influencers to promote the brand.

4. Activity: The frequency with which influencer posts or comments and their overall activity play an important role in influencing the target as it predicts a potential impact before a campaign is started.

While influence marketing is commonly used as a strategy for consumer brands and their associations, such techniques and features are better for social enterprise marketing; credibility campaigns for influencers will not achieve their advertising objectives if the public is aware that influencers are paid for. It is, therefore, very important to work with people who have a true passion for your project. This only shows how incredibly genuine the secret to an effective influencer campaign is. Influencer marketing and social businesses are ideal for authenticity as potentially targeted influencers are often already aware of the causes they support. This simplifies their recognition, allows a better relationship to be formed, and makes your message more organic.

Strategic Planning

It is always very important to have a clear view of what you intend to achieve, particularly for social companies, before participating in any influencing venture. Furthermore, the method of achieving these goals and the degree to which success is measured is of equal significance. The tactical analyzes contribute to informed decisions on issues of importance, such as mediums most important to the consumer market and whether the main goal is to share brand content with as many people as possible or to participate in creating new content in order to connect people deeply. Early participation with influencers is advisable to look for opinions on how the partnership works best.

Targeting Relevant audiences

Statistics and experience have proved that engaging individuals and people with the largest social media and fan base to support your mission does not necessarily guarantee the best results. Statistics, however, say that niche media influencers generally show smaller follow-ups for more public engagement and the highest conversion rates. Often known as micro-influencers, these individuals have a highly targeted and interactive online audience. Inspired marketing by micro-influencers for non-profits and other social enterprises has impeccable results. These micro-influencers are passionate supporters of their brands and play important roles in awareness and in driving valuable activity.

Measurement of productivity

The ability to quantify the success of marketing campaigns was and still is a major challenge today. It is hardly anybody else to understand why surveys show that calculating the return on investment (ROI) of influencer marketing is the biggest challenge they face. To address this challenge, a wide range of metrics, such as engagement of the audience, feelings, and changes could begin to make sure that more is measured than just fan numbers.

In order to support this significant attempt to evaluate progress to influencer marketing campaigns, crowdfunding consultancy, non-profit advisory, and profit consulting services would, more specifically, encourage social organizations to create dedicated fundraising pages for each of its influencers. It provides a unique forum through which the ties to their networks can be created, demonstrates the direct dollar value of each influencer's contribution, and provides a way to determine the partnership's effectiveness.

Legal boundaries

Understanding the laws of partnership agreements between influencers and firms is crucial. While some influencers promote many social business causes without charge, most influencers with highly trained individuals often require payments to safeguard their official partnerships.

Marketing influencers revolutionize the business world in general and has the potential to optimize marketing for social enterprises.

Tools of Weapons and Marketing of Influence

You need to turbo-charge all aspects before you can have your ultimate, sophisticated company. Use the seven key marketing tools and the six influential weapons.

Here below I will describe each of the seven main marketing tools and briefly clarify them. It is important to be aware that once these seven main devices are set up and run by mechanics, the message should motivate readers to take the action they want. In this chapter I will introduce briefly these six main prominent weapons. It is the combination of the marketing mechanics, who are the seven key marketing instruments, and the message principles, which are the arms of influence that enable you to succeed!

Here are the seven main marketing tools.

Tool 1. Advertising. If you have the budget for it, marketing has the largest scope and generates the highest level of awareness. Here's what you need to do to create high-response publicity. Be distinguished. Capture attention with a shouting headline. Once your headline hooks, you have to keep the copy or text in the body of your ad reading. Make sure a call to action is included.

Tool 2. Registered mail. A successful direct mail campaign depends on your mailings being regular and consistent. First, use as much light as you can. Second, placed the envelopes with messages. Third, consider how you sort your own mail to increase the chances that the envelope will be opened. Use direct mail as a weapon to attack your dream prospects.

Tool 3. Business literature. Consider corporate literature as your direct mail. Your brochures will draw from your practice marketing efforts and be a miniature version of your pitch or key story. However, it must keep in mind that facts tell, but stories sell. Use the same graphics you use in your presentations, publicity, and direct mail to improve your marketing efforts.

Tool 4. Public relations. If you organize exciting events such as trade show parties and benefits for your customers, you do business relationships. PR also includes press releases, builds news connections to write segments about you, and has strong forces to help you, such as business associations and community groups. Most enterprises have cohesive, very effective public relations effort, yet they can work miracles to build your fame, even if you are a small business.

Tool 5. Personal contact. Personal contact is the most powerful form of marketing and often has good conversations with your prospects.

Tool 6. Trade shows and education in the market. Trade shows are a great way to provide your prospects with product and market information. When done correctly, it can take you in a single event from darkness to the top of the market. If not done correctly, it could be a great waste of money. To have a great trade show, follow these three rules:

1. Get noticed.

2. Pass traffic. Drive traffic.

3. Find leads. Follow leads.

Tool 7. Internet. The Internet can give your business a great opportunity, or it can become your worst caution overnight if some competitor learns how to use it better than you. Amazon, for example, struggled in the early years but still took $1B of other booksellers' market share. Because Amazon grew on the Internet, sales in four years reached $1B. Before the Internet, it took 50 years for other bookshop chains to sell $1B. Here are the five key Internet activities:

1. Find leads. Follow leads.

2. Build a connection.

3. Interact to the greatest extent possible.

4. Provide a webinar.

5. Transform traffic into sales.

All these key marketing tools need to work together. Naturally, you should be consistent with your content and your message, and all duplicated, or syndicated content should be referenced in some way.

Here are a few important questions to ask in order to ensure that key marketing tools are effective. Are all segments on your website? Is it available for download? Are they available to visitors to your site, so that visitors can share and mail to others? Is your content contributing to your business? Do you offer free training as a way to create your leadership list?

As mentioned at the beginning of this segment, it is important to use the influential weapons (including in their contents, pitch, and storyboard) to get them to act.

To help you realize the power of persuasion guns, do you feel like you are an easy mark on peddlers' or fundraisers' pitches? Do you have unused subscriptions to newspapers or tickets to different charity events? Why an application in a certain way is rejected when a request in a slightly different way for the same favor is successful? The key is the psychology of persuasion, sometimes called influential weapons.

Here are the 6 influential Weapons of Impact that will help your influence on people:

Way 1. Reciprocity. This rule is an old rule and says that we should try to reimburse what another person has given us in kind.

Way 2. Engagement and coherence. Like other influential weapons, this rule is our will to be and appear to be in keeping with what we already did. For example, if we buy a small item, then we are often asked whether we want to over-size it or buy another item for a further 50 percent (as an example), all of them presented to us at the same time. This is part of the process of upselling.

Way 3. Social facts. Social proofs. This rule says that when we know what other people think is correct, we determine what is correct. In other words, we conclude that we will make fewer mistakes by behaving in accordance with social evidence than against it. This is why the proof of a product is so popular; they make us think that if all the people in the comments like or use the product, how can we be wrong to use the product as well.

Way 4. Liking. This rule is based on the fact that most of us would like to say yes to the demands of anyone we know and like. Either positive or serious, the prospects are more likely to be purchased from a salesperson if the salesperson is similar in age, gender, ethnicity, politics, and several other factors such as leisure and even work.

Way 5. Authority. We are trained from birth to be correct in obedience to proper authority and wrong in disobedience. This message is conveyed in the legal, medical, military, and political systems that we as adults meet. Advertisers often use the popularity and power of doctors in our society to employ actors to play the part of a physician and speak about a brand positively. The message from the physician, an official, can influence prospects to buy the product.

Way 6. Scarcity. When we learn that it will soon become unavailable, the call for something of interest grows. This is based on the scarcity principle. There is a secondary power or influence source with the principle of scarcity. With fewer opportunities available, we lose our freedoms and hate to lose our liberties. If the free choice is limited because of the scarcity of something, the need to maintain our freedom makes us want it more than we did before.

By understanding and using these weapons, you can achieve a distinct automatic, mindless compliance from people who are willing to say yes without first thinking.

With the ever-accelerating pace and information crush of today's life, this type of hypnotic writing that creates unexpected conformity is becoming increasingly common.

It will, therefore, be important to understand why the use of these weapons of influence means your public will be automatically persuaded.

Network Marketing Success - Leadership is Influence

A leader is a person who will do everything she/he can to 'transform' his downlines to do what he needs to do to succeed in his marketing network. Now, there will no doubt be people who just aren't prepared to 'do whatever is necessary', probably because they say to themselves that it's too hard, they just can't do it, or anything. But a leader will be able to persuade, excite, and encourage more people to turn, improve, and develop skills, etc. than the less influential person.

If you have no power, you cannot lead others in any way. This assertion begs the question... 'How else do you evaluate influence? ' I'm going to give you a story to answer that question...

Two events took place in less than a week behind in 1996 and they shocked the world: the deaths of Princess Diana and Mother Teresa. Such two women could not have been more different on the surface. Diana was a tall, attractive young English princess mixed in the highest society. Mother Teresa, the winner of the Nobel Peace Prize, was a little Catholic elderly now born in Albania who served in extreme poverty in Calcutta,

India. The extraordinary thing, however, was that their impact was strikingly alike. In a sample published in 1996 by the London Daily Mail, Princess Diana and Mother Teresa were voted the most caring people on earth in 1st and 2nd place.

How can someone like Diana ever look the same as Mother Teresa? She demonstrated the strength of 'influence'.

When Prince Charles was married, almost 1 billion people attended the wedding ceremony on television. Upon spending a little time in her new job, she started to travel to and represent the royal family all around the world and quickly made it her mission to work for others who are less fortunate than her, raising money for many charitable causes. Throughout this process, she established innumerable important relationships... politicians, humanitarian leaders, entertainers and heads of state, etc. In the early stages, she was essentially a catalyst for fundraising, but over time she expanded her influence... she inspired changes.

She brought people together for causes, including AIDS research, leprosy treatment, and landmines ban. She brought that last issue to world leaders' attention, even persuaded the Clinton administration to champion a global conference outlawing the landmines and aiding their victims. Her influence was so strong that she put the issue on the world agenda and even influenced the US President.

Initially, Diana's name provided her with a platform for talking to others, but she quickly became an influential person regardless of her title. She may well have lost her title designation after she was divorced from Charles in 1996, but her power (read 'influence') in others still continued to rise.... while... regardless of titles and place, that of the ex-husband Charles was gradually less. Amazingly, her influence continued even after her tragic death. When her funeral was broadcast on TV and radio, the total audience of watching and listening was estimated to be about 2.5 billion... far over twice the number of people who joined her wedding. A classic proof of the 'influence' law.

Diana is probably not known as a leader ever... but that's exactly what she was. She did things because she was an influencer, and leadership is power, nothing more, nothing less.

Leadership is NOT: Management... usually comes with some kind of title, but a title is not required for influence. A manager can continue with direction; however, if they are also a leader, they can't change it. It will be important to reorient people in a new direction.

Information... Knowledge... It is difficult for an "average person" to understand... but whose ability to conduct is so small it hardly even registers on a scale. There are many exceptionally educated and well-informed people.

Contractor... You could be unusually inventive, innovative, successful, outstanding salesman, etc... but you have no influence on people in the long term. Not all managers are businessmen, and not all managers are rulers.

Pioneer... It's a mistake to assume that anyone is necessarily a leader "outside the front". First and foremost, being a leader is different. To be a leader, one should not only be outside but have people come back willingly and follow the lead, acting on the dream of leaders.

Leadership and rank have nothing to do with one another. Some people have a "ranking", but have little or no influence, and many people have no rank at all but are highly influential. "Leadership is not apposition or a title, it is action and example."

A proverb of leadership: "Whoever thinks he leads but does not follow, just walks." If you cannot influence people, they will not follow you. And you're not a leader if they don't follow. This is the 'Law of Influence.'

Regardless of how you imagine and talk about yourself, a truly successful leader is someone who encourages you to achieve your network marketing success. You have to train your down lines to find your own leads and your own perspectives... both offline and online.

You must inspire others as a leader. A leader of the first class is not a person who does it all by himself, but who teaches others to be self-religious and to be able to replace you entirely. The biggest position you can find is where you're not needed anymore.

You will also know that you are not their boss, threatening or giving orders. People don't join the network advertising to be regulated by their own businesses, but to be independent companies. You can learn to be firm if you want to make something for your own performance, but you can be steadfast in inspiring... not bossing.

Finally, someone who wants to serve and make sacrifices is a good marketing leader in the network. There is no long-term network marketing success without commitment, and even if sometimes it will ask to give your time, resources and sometimes your comfort, it will pay off if you work wisely and build a stable team so that your downline members are willing to double what they saw and heard you.

Some of my fundamental values:

1. You must really want to help people... you can't counterfeit it. People know.

2. This is a friendship, mentoring, coaching... not a sales company.

3. People come into PEOPLE, not a company, not a compensation package, not a brand.

4. Prospects want to know... Can I? & Could you assist me?

5. People remember only those who matter... so I want to care for you and support you.

6. Top priority... help people make their dreams come true.

CHAPTER FIVE

The Keys to Influence in Social Marketing

The aim of this section is to correlate the findings of 'influence' and social marketing, i.e., to create an effective tool for social networking.

Until we migrate on, I want to make sure that this content and 'Influence' information are not intended to manipulate a person to buy or do something that they would not buy or do otherwise. The data is designed to help anyone who markets or sells a service or knows how best to deliver it.

Key Influence #1: Reciprocation: This core is pre-questioned to give. The basic values of human culture are expressed in the main reciprocation. Reciprocation states that a person wants to recover what someone else gave them.

How can social marketing work?

You could provide a complimentary report.

You can provide appropriate and concise answers or guidance on posted questions.

You may connect to a great chapter. Any such methods enflame the law of reciprocation. Once, however, please note that the goal was to help first. If you help in order to get back, you will be doomed. The reciprocation rule works if the individual is unconditional.

Key Influence #2: Commitment and Consistency: Many other people would like to have their words, beliefs, and actions to be consistent and perceived. Consistent behavior offers a beneficial approach to life. A consistent alignment provides a shortcut through the labyrinth of the present day. In so far as commitment, a decision (the purchasing commitment) is usually taken on an emotional and then supported by logic. The greater the commitment, the greater the reasoning after the commitment has been made.

It is essential to be consistent with ALL your information in social marketing: you send your image to ALL your social sites Your Twits You are active off-line. Yes, even this must be consistent; otherwise, it will "pull" into your digital world to help people to make their bid. You will need to discuss and solve your emotional "needs" and provide sufficient evidence to support their decision-making. In the first place, the facts will help the average person to commit to your offer. Combining the emotional problem with reality is, however, a powerful combination.

Key influence #3: Social evidence: This influence basically means that people observe and do what others do. There are two main circumstances when this aspect is important: when people are unsure about a situation, they are more likely to see what others do.

The second is if an individual is the same. The trend is to follow a person's actions with similarities.

I believe that worldwide economic conditions can be described as 'uncertain', and so it is to the advantage of a social marketer to use this uncertainty and to post information supported by its services. Ideally, this data should come from sources from third parties to improve credibility.

So, as people start to take action on the bid, others like that will see it as the right step to take and use the same deal.

Key Influence #4: Liking: the influence is important... people prefer to say yes to someone they like.

Similarity increase physical attractiveness and repeated exposure–no... not such exposure:-)!

Positive partnership. i.e., Fan of the same team. This influence is central to social marketing to create liability in some respects. This is done through photos and information about favorite activates and teams or organizations.

Instead, remind potential customers frequently to learn more about you by "following" you and creating the like connection.

Key influence #5: Authority: Several studies have demonstrated the desire to comply with authority in our society. An authority figure might wear a 'white coat', a uniform, or a sequence of initials. One explanation for this is that the authority leader holds a high degree of skill, experience, knowledge, and energy.

It is interesting that there are three kinds of symbols in research that are accepted as authoritative in the social field: Title, automobile, clothing. So how can a person apply this information to social marketing?

Use your title letters, i.e., if you are a certified personal trainer, use 'CPT', when you post a picture of "professional" clothing, then you're given a title. Of course, "professional" clothing depends on the industry, so I believe that a Speedo isn't a professional salesman... or then... just keep the image as real you are. If you've got a great car, why not pose in professional clothing in front of you.

Creating and Implementing a Marketing Plan

The first of the year is a perfect time to carry out a marketing plan. The marketing plan is the main basis for the business, there is no business without customers or clients. A marketing plan will have the same process as any other (long-term) strategic plan: set objectives, establish an action, plan to implement objectives, and reassess the effectiveness of action taken. If you don't make a marketing strategy before (or a development plan of any sort), it's important to get something on paper and get started. The plan could be corrected, supplemented and evaluated after implementation, but nothing is helpful before implementation. Do not let cognitive pause intervention paralysis take place.

Set reasonable, realistic, and measurable marketing goals in the relevant areas. Determine and describe an ideal client or company. Do that from personal experience and what is apparent in the business. Current customers, sales centers, networking, and principal customer or company retention are primary areas of concern in the marketing plan.

Find the complexities of the business in general. What is the essence of the business or consumer demand? Is it elastic, where competition exists, and prices have a major impact on sales or inelastic, where an increase in prices does not drastically decrease sales? In the last year, what has changed? Have customer or product expectations changed? Determine and define the profile for the ideal consumer or client. What power centers do the perfect consumer or company have? Identify all last year's reference sources. Does the description of the ideal customer or customer suggest that reference sources do not send references to the company? If so, identify the sources of reference.

With respect to consumer or product referrals, consider increasing the percentage of customers you refer to. What is the actual percentage of customers who refer? Set an objective based on past results and develop a method to monitor the achievement of that objective.

Influence centers are resources that can provide new customers with a sustainable source. Consider establishing a relationship with a certain number of influential centers in the following year. Who are the influential centers for your marketing? How many are you connected with? Set an objective based on past results and devise a method to monitor the achievement of this objective.

Networking involves the Web and face to face communications aimed at portraying the organization and its leadership as a professional and responsible member of the enterprise community. The networking activity enables information to be shared in the business community, which can be of benefit to the company through the establishment of its skills and integrity. Consider the aim to participate effectively in community and information activities, which improve the reputation of the company. Develop a way to monitor new activities attracted or enabled by networking.

For a potential customer who is known, consider the objective of gaining that customer within a fixed period.

List the measures to be taken to achieve the goal for each objective. For example, consider developing a referral system using thank you cards, surveys or meetings for customer or customer refers; use special events (dinner or social events) to keep up with clients or customers and create opportunities to introduce friends or relatives to the business, or provide information through schedule news and newsletters. Suggest identifying gatherings where new influence centers can come together, join alliances with influential centers, give a talk to meetings or write publications for influential centers, and use social networking sites to access and recognize influential centers. For networking, consider developing effective marketing collateral including business cards, business information brochures, information about the company and their stories, product or services features and capacity brochures and information; publicity in the appropriate locations; the use of direct mail, as appropriate. Consider sending direct mail to specific clients or customers, initiating social activities with the potential client, and supplying the potential customer with information tools.

In order to prioritize the project, list the targets with the measures to be taken in the left column of the table. List the months of the year in the top row of the table in the columns that follow. Place an x for this activity every month in which an action is to be taken. After all, activities have been completed, replace the x with the cost of the operation each month. For instance, when an activity is to join the Chamber of Commerce, the initial month may include the cost of annual duties and estimates of incidental costs involved in participating in certain activities may be provided during the following months. Once all xs are replaced with numbers, the columns should be summed up for each month, and each activity row should have a total column run.

To execute the program, create a promotional calendar on the days of the month in which activities will start and be completed. Assess the necessary dates, remembering that what is actually created is a checklist, not a calendar. Monitor the plan to ensure that customer information is gathered to determine the source of new customers. The execution of the program and its success is reviewed regularly.

Now that the vital strategic plan for a company, the marketing plan, and the performance of the plan depends on compliance with the plan and on analysis of the plan, as evaluation reveals the most successful actions to achieve the objectives.

The Power of Influence in Marketing

Influence is one's ability to exert power over other people's minds. People who are extremely influential can convince someone or something and cause changes. To understand the art of manipulating people, you have to discover what influences them already. One has to learn how to walk before running, which imitates the above concept. And precisely what makes people victims of the forces of influence? What do they use to be lacking for everyone else? We must understand several concepts when we try to change people's thinking and behavior. However, the difficulty is how we know people who visit our websites, especially in the online community. After all, it's only a point on our stat bar graph or only a number on our traffic counter. How should you affect these people without meeting them physically?

You read the right segment if you can't answer this question. It's not as difficult as you think, but not as easy as we elude, so just take mental notes. The general response is to identify and analyze the general patterns of human behavior or thinking. These patterns help you to understand how people work. You know these trends to influence people around you. That's exactly why you don't need to know everyone to figure out what drives them to buy or do. A lot of this became apparent to me after taking neural and social psychology courses, and I want to share my knowledge with you. Nonetheless, before we apply it to the online marketing environment, it is important to look at the dynamics of the brain.

In neural psychology, has been examined in greater detail the various parts of the brain and its function. It has been analyzed the Triune Brain Model. Paul MacLean created the theory to explain how the human brain has evolved throughout history. This theory is based on the three compounds of the Triune brain: Old brain, the Midbrain, and New brain. The old brain is known as the reptile brain, which focuses mainly on your survival. It takes one's situation into account and identifies and perceives any potential threats or benefits. It also regulates autonomous functions such as heartbeats, respiration, digestion, and movement. The midbrain, also known as the limbic system, is responsible mainly for feelings, memories, and focus.

Our emotions produce positive or negative feelings. The new brain, also known as the neo-cortex, controls logical processes like rational thinking, thinking skills, language, and speech processing. For all cognitive processes, where the midbrain and the old brain deal with unaware processes, our neo-cortex is responsible. Believe it or not, most of the processings go through our unconscious channel and therefore lead to automatic emotions, reactions, etc. The unconscious part of our brain also aids the new brain in prioritizing certain conscious activities. So, if our thinking is largely unconscious, how can we, as marketers, tap into something that is uncontrollable? What should your advertising platform or portal look like to optimize the subconscious feedback of a customer that could lead to potentially output-equivalent sales?

A) Show some sort of grading scale of products in which visitors can comment on these reviews. Grading systems work because people think the product is good and valid if someone else has commented/validated it. People never depend on themselves when they divulge into unfamiliar territory, so they look at others when they decide what to do. Why? It's a natural tendency for a person to try and fit the social standard, as confirmed by the presence of the scale. One might find this much more profitable than ad banners because the reviews and ratings are personal. People feel comfortable because they realize another person is writing a review on the other side of the screen, in comparison to the machine-controlled ad banners.

B) First of all, this dimension is extremely important because it is the first matter that the visitor analyzes consciously and unconsciously. When you try to direct your visitors to a specific product, make certain that the product is the first thing they see and is unmistakable. Research by a watch marketing company found that a one-watch ad on the front page converted nine times sales to an ad page that provided visitors with a selection of 9 different watches. Why? It is simple. Giving them more options would lead to more confusion and will not make a choice. The key is, therefore, to guide the right of the visitor to your product. Take a look today at any successful marketing campaign, and you will see what we mean.

C) Elude that a product is nearly gone or is in limited quantity. The simple principle of life to always remember is that people will always want what they cannot have or know in small quantities, whether it comes to people or products. Why is it working? The main reason for this is that they are happy to achieve something that is confined to the general public. This makes the person feel superior to those who can't land such an item. It's a very common tactic and behaves like a charm. We saw one recently for a product called "Guru Blueprint", which revealed it would only be available for one week, and then the item would be deleted. Thumb rule: If something makes you money, why would you take this product off the internet in your right mind. This tactic is intended to generate hype and to convert sales as quickly as possible. I can guarantee that the "Guru Blueprint" will be up again, especially if it makes a nice coin to its owner.

D) Building a relationship by offering something away. This is my personal favorite since this is a big part of why we have experienced so much online success. It automatically triggers a feeling of being indebted to that person when someone gives you something. To get rid of this feeling, you unconsciously want to get rid of it by returning something, whether it's by supporting yourself as an affiliate or buying your real product. A perfect example is when someone gives free e-books, plugins, etc. This makes it especially useful when we want someone to join our mailing list, providing them with a free e-book that includes enough information to make it appropriate, but never enough to be unsubscribed too. We still have people who do not subscribe, but the ratio is very much in favor. It should also be remembered that people can never get enough. When you give information via email to people, make sure it's important and correct, because people will respect it more and want more.

E) Personalize your posts to make sure that you convey that the brand is for you by using the word "you". The point is that the person feels the product is more personalized. Also, make your language comfortable, write it as you speak to them, because the more personalized the writing, the better it will be.

F) Use your own facts or stories, because the consumer will typically use stories in the marketing letter to illustrate how to avoid a financial disaster from buying that particular product. We read or hear the story, making our brains respond as if we had the same experience. In fact, storytelling is a perfect way to convince a person because, once done correctly, he/she loses his ability to think rationally. Because you are emotionally immersed in your story and deciding whether or not you want to witness your success or stop one of your failures.

CHAPTER SIX

Understanding Your Content Marketing Success

As you start looking back this year and find out what has worked and what hasn't worked out, you should know what the factors for the success of your Strategy have been and what it has been like.

It is quite important with all the effort and time that you put into your content marketing strategy that you understand clearly how you measure the success of your Strategy and how well you actually do it. You should look at the approach from a broader perspective, taking the picture into account. Your content marketing strategy should involve your audience and increase your business revenue.

The questions you should ask to work out a study, review, or creative project is first to ask relevant questions which you've arranged in a way that works for you. The answers to the questions help you to understand which parts of your strategy work and which parts need to be tweaked.

Is the data you use important to your content marketing strategy? If your content addresses the problems of the people you try to reach, your Strategy is relevant for your company. Your Strategy works if you have been able to achieve your professional goals. You can look at your audience and compare them to some of your metrics, such as likes, web site visits, retweets, references, and conversion rates if you are not sure the answer is provided.

Is your content marketing universally consistent? You will have to be consistent with how you convey data if your content marketing is to be effective. Your audience must be able to count on a constant flow of information, and the type of information must be present if they expect it. This is one way you build confidence with your audience. A metric for this is how you are reliant on sharing your content to build opportunities and retain your existing customers. If you are good at being reliable, you must follow a consistent schedule (an editorial calendar will help greatly) and make sure you have a full commitment to your posting schedule.

Can you get your audience involved? You are effective in engaging the audience if your content is entertaining, insightful, educational, and convincing. It is important for you to write stories that your audience can relate to. If the content touches your audience emotionally, they will want to interact with you and read anything you post. Naturally, when it comes to writing top quality material, your particular voice is significant. It may change over time, but whatever you choose it is your voice.

Are you using wisely your time? You have to ensure that your content marketing campaign is time-consuming. Before you do anything, it's important to have a process in place. If you don't, you could face frustration and a lot of wheel spinning and stress. When you work effectively, it ensures that you can efficiently delegate tasks, pick great topics, and achieve what you want to do in a timely manner. You most likely don't use your time wisely, if you find it difficult to reach your deadlines, do many things at the last minute, rewrite material a lot of the time, etc.

Has your level of influence improved positively? It can seem like power is difficult to measure, but it really isn't that difficult. It is possible that the actual measurements may vary over time, but there will always be influences (if you work on them). Influence is a wide attribute and should be seen over a long time. If you do a good job, you should see positive progress from month to month in your impact.

Is your content compatible with the goals you have set? Your content strategy should support all of your business objectives (long-term as well as short-term). It is crucial that you are not concerned with meeting deadlines because they can actually prevent you from completing the particular project you are working on.

Implementation. You must implement your Strategy now that you have successfully asked and answered important questions. There are a few tips that will certainly help you.

Share your answers with your staff: Sharing your data with your staff is an excellent idea. The information should always be in front of you so that you can refer to it. It ought to be your bible.

Make your own assessment: you should rate the marketing of your own content. You can use a scale of 1 to 5 where "1" is "very good," and "5" is "very unsatisfactory," and after the material has been analyzed, you can summarize it, and easily identify the strengths and weaknesses of your approach. Then you can tweak accordingly. Use the information to identify patterns and trends.

The significance of feedback is critical for your company. You won't know where you need to improve without feedback. It is, therefore, extremely important that you measure your results against your competitors' results. It is a good idea to try to find missing information and details not applicable to what you are trying to achieve.

There is no point in putting together and executing a content marketing plan if you just let it go after that. You must work as hard as you can to get your content viral. You have to find out if it works and if it doesn't work, you have to figure out how to make it better. In a competitive market, you need to take advantage of any information you can to help you compete.

Youth Marketing in the Broadband Era

PHENOMENON: Young people are more educated than advertisers.

Many Asian consumer electronics vendors were sued at the global launch of Sony's PSP. It was Sony's duty to take this action since young people and other enthusiastic gamers, in particular from Europe, saw their PSPs getting in the summer of 2005, while PSP was not launched until autumn of 2005. Consumers placed their orders via the Internet, and the goods were sent to gamers through global delivery channels. These companies threatened Sony's distribution and launch strategy. The question remains: Was it really worth that kind of legal counterpunch? Are similar cases going to become part of our global business reality?

It is increasingly difficult to reach and influence the young-minded audience. The patterns of consumption shift from mass media to micro media for the masses. Savvy media-driven consumers, often under the age of 25, are influenced by global trends. The knowledge and adjustment of these trends are sometimes even faster than local marketers can put their products on the market. The broadband accelerated Internet is at the core of this innovative action.

Global consumption at first glance seems to be good news for marketers: global marketing, quick localization of campaigns, self-employment by consumers, and, therefore, fewer resources for home promotions. Is this really so, however? For many brands, marketing to empowered young people is both a dream and a nightmare. For example, knowledge about features, design, and usabilities like product bugs and negative experiences fly the world over networks just as quickly as the trends themselves. Consumers can adjust to any product's global opinion databases 24 hours a day. The internet-enabled user has more perfect market knowledge than ever and is increasingly aware of their new powers.

Since rumors and experiences spring from one country to another, the message originally tried by the brand's agency is not uninfluenced. Marketers lose control of their campaign messages easily. In our wireless world, repairing this damage with local initiatives such as when a product receives negative feedback from consumers can be a major challenge. For instance, Kryptonite, a famous lock manufacturer, had to spend a substantial part of its marketing budget on business some years ago, following instructions posted on the online site showing how easy it is to open Kryptonite locks with a simple ballpoint pen.

Modern marketing is about creating a useful and sustainable brand-segment dialogue. I suggest that marketers must switch from one-way push-marketing to listening more closely to their target groups and to be prepared to communicate with the target group in a way that encourages them to be part of the product experience. In addition, if an average Western customer living in one city is subjected to more than 3,500 to 5,000 marketing messages every day, I argue strongly that discovering the means and methods for breaking the constantly growing barrier is more than necessary. I see this hurdle not only with traditional marketing methods but also with new approaches.

Behavior: I'm alive – I am on @facebook @instagram @twitter @pinterest etc. – get in touch with me!

There are more than 600 million internet users available worldwide, compared with about 200 million they were in 2005. So, who knows more about numbers? Who cares if it will be 600 million users or 400 million or 800 million people on broadband? Offline vs. Online–couldn't care less–the target in the new mass location is all about hitting. Here's online life–and the markets are huge. The group of young people is obviously the most experienced and knowledgeable on digital channels. They grew up with them, and these channels play a natural role every day in their lives.

If you look more closely at the young-minded segment's online presence, the findings are compelling. More than 89% of the 18-24 age group were online in the US at the end of 2019, and more than 85% were online for over three years. Europe is lagging a little behind, but the trend is clear. There is only one thing a company should draw-to have an online campaign is a must!

In addition, 12-17-year-old internet users say that email is best used to talk with parents or institutions but more likely to use instant message when talking to one another. This is reflected even in common words: "Online on @Facebook @Instagram @twitter" is a common status of living amongst your peers.

Generation C (C= Content) creates the content of its own with Smartphones and PCs and makes it available via dedicated sites or Peer-to-Peer networks to its peers. Whereas baby boomers (born before 1960) had to learn what mass media was, and Generation X (born 1960-1975) has evolved from television and first-generation video games (and now concentrates on their happy family lives with high debt ratios), the Next / Idols / Content member of the new generation (born after 1975) is a multi-task media born. If traditional channels do not meet their own preferences, there is always an alternative: online service.

The new content-on-demand is somewhat like a Pandora's box. When opened, consumers learn that the amount of content within their preferences is basically unlimited. Consumers will no longer be happy and satisfied with the content that media companies provide to them. You want to control, get what you want–anywhere, now. And they ask the media company to do so, which is now struggling with lower profits–not easy equitation. Look at the falling sales figures of the music industry and the reality of more music than ever available. Who loses, who wins? Losing gatekeepers, winning consumers? The "long tail" effect makes more streams possible than the few media conglomerates offer. Outside music chart and mainstream films, we will see more popular performances and peer group stars.

Young people are much more heterogeneous than stable "30-somethings" with families and children in their advertising needs. Youngsters find/define their own identity/independence continuously. The needs of 14 years of age differ greatly from those of 18 years of age. Subcultures (skaters, goths, mangas, Sudocu musicians, ravers, etc.) and association with strong leaders of opinion (pop stars, celebrities, sports stars) convey this desire for identity. If a marketer wishes to segment the youth market, patterns, and subcultures within ages and genders should be differentiated carefully.

Brands (Pepsi and Britney Spears) need a deep, long-term commitment to genuine youth credibility if they are affiliated with subcultures (skateboarding/snowboarding/ DJ-ing / grafiti) or artists. This can be achieved only if the pairs and places where the segment naturally moves and meets are positively credible. A brand never should claim to be a child, if not. The way young people communicate is special and pretends to be obvious. The biggest thing a company can draw to itself is an enticing end-user audience, like the fantastic user base of Apple and the incredible popularity of MTV since the 1980s.

The digital channels win over the time and focus of the youth segment. They are, therefore, extremely important to marketers. Even in early 2000, the key role played by digital channels of interaction was to support other networks, such as print or TV. Now it seems that TV, radio, and print media are like "Gateways" to digital channels at the dawn of the internet era. Forum discussions already use viral marketing. There are not enough solutions to traditional advertising approaches (including Web publicity, email marketing, and search marketing).

There is no question of whether or not virtual platforms should be used, but what other channels should be used to bring traffic to the online site.

The varied digital communication and channels methods continue to be difficult for advertisers. The function of digital channels is essential when they enable communication between group members or when they allow icons to be projected. In other words, communicating between members of the target group is one of the main success factors in youth marketing. It is important to note that today, most of the largest online brands are digital channels themselves.

Marketers need alternative means of advertising: alternative ways of communicating their message to young people and beyond are important. Digital services can be the best digital marketing rather than advertising. However, not everything must be digital, and people still value tangible things. Digital platforms allow youth to do "things" (e.g., they are able to get, make, share, and influence things that are important to them in a certain place and/or time. Additionally, marketers can listen to their target groups through digital channels—interactivity is the essence of these channels. Human behavior and limitations are not applicable in this world. Anything is possible. So why even the most modern marketers stick to a game like a billboard, a static ad, or anything? "Dear Mr. Brand! Hi! The world there is different!". This new virtual environment can also affect the experience of the real world by a player. Online and computer games are not just a "small hobby region for children", they contributed to approximately 120 billion € in 2018. Look at the rules of gaming. Maybe they were the rules of modern marketing—for and with your brand, what would you do in this world? Can the best means of contemporary marketing emerge from the multicomplex world of game design in a manner similar to how interactive marketing started out in the mid-1990s when the digital channel was born?

Advertisers need to invest in their creative activities. It's nice to have and sponsor an event. Nonetheless, to make a lasting impression among participants of the music festival, for example, they have to engage with the company. The use of digital channels is the key to building event experiences for participants before and after the event. Separations, especially the young, try new things more openly when the product involves more–touch, feel smell, experience–but use digital means to extend it beyond conventional ones.

RECOMMENDATIONS: What could function?

In conclusion, I have listed below a number of recommendations to modern marketers in modern marketing planning. Such best practices reach beyond the youth group, which in turn are the main variables for new, desirable, and impact-oriented marketing activities. In addition, there is no brand that should not rethink the impact on their brand positions on the Internet.

1. BE INNOVATIVE, and DARE TRY OUT: Testing and error are the best way to understand the emerging channels. Exploration rounds gain knowledge of how customers are behaving. In marketed preparation, experimental and various test methods are needed, while measurement and metrics are collected in the execution process. But training takes place more and more by trying and making mistakes. Allow mistakes, then, but learn from them!

2. ACTIVATE THE LOGICAL SIDE OF ADVERTISING: Advertising goes beyond innovative ideas–administrators are constantly pursuing advertising profits. It is better possible to trace and calculate marketing effects on the digital channel than on any other channel. We are committed to a system where promotional measures should be carefully planned, and innovative ideas are usually included in traditional advertising networks. We can see that marketers should do much more to ensure that interaction motivates the group to take action.

3. BUILD BEHAVIOURAL KNOW-HOW: Target groups hopping from one medium to another more than ever. Wherever the target group is, it is important to be present. As the digital channel plays an important role in modern behavior, any corporate scheme should be highly important. Knowing the behavior of a target group and developing your digital service on its basis, is the key to online success.

4. LEADERS OPINION BRING CREDIBILITY: Each community of peers is affected by its members. Particularly for the young category, the target group includes leaders and extends events into virtual space by creating interactions before and after. Allow creative use of the mobile platform with leading consumer brands and note even offline on the market.

5. LISTENING AND NETWORKING: Knowing the networking landscape is essential to effective communication with your target group. A good marketer has to attempt to listen and respond—it's not a matter of pushing but listening. Relations are built across the creative spectrum of relevant media outlets with demanding target audiences, such as youngsters. Creating online communities and providing natural networking resources can help a brand grow closer to young people.

6. PARTNERING: Strive to pursue new approaches and work closely with partners. It's not about trying to do something alone—other brands face the same challenges. Why not consider reliable partners to advance one's own objectives? It all involves increased openness, debate, and trials with various types of partners. For the youth group, advertising with partners that are reputable for the segment is of the utmost importance. Find and work for them!

7. FRESH AND EXCLUSIVE: Brands should be increasingly exclusive. The objective should be to increase regular visitors by offering new, up-to-date, and attractive content. Investments in the development and creativity of one's own IPR (Intellectual property rights) can be very effective. The digital environment allows faster reactions and starts than any previous stream.

8. *DEVELOP SUSTAINABILITY INTERACTIONS:* brands are to set up a dedicated channel for communications in their segments. Its correspondence platform is much stronger than transitional online campaigns. In this type of marketing-oriented online service, the content should be based on specific areas of interest to create a communication arena more like a media channel operation than a marketer-only operation.

Rev-Up Your Social Media Marketing Strategy

Social media also revolutionized not only our language of communication but our way of conducting business. The dizzying impact of 24-hour unrestricted access to people and data has turned various tools into a game-changer.

There is a broad and growing list of websites, including YouTube, Instagram, Flickr, Pinterest, Twitter, Tumblr, LinkedIn, and Facebook. For business entrepreneurs and professionals, these social destinations have turned golf into a 'C-suite powerbrokers' opportunity to strategically network and close deals based on shared interests and personal commitment. However, these sites do more by providing users with valuable property to services or advertise products, expand and create brand recognition and feedback, build relationships, and build community forums. In fact, customers, industry experts, prospective clients, hiring managers, and prospects have unfettered access.

Therefore, social media level the playing field by giving anyone access without time, location, or social status restrictions.

The first foray into social media can be intimidating and disconcerting. Newcomers to the room might wonder: who reads? Am I going to be heard or noticed? Isn't anything fun and games? Is it not invasive? It takes time, persistence, and a work-smart, unheard approach to make an effort worthwhile. Whether you are an entrepreneur or a businessperson, the advertising performance of your products, businesses, or your personal brand is decided by your interest in the various platforms.

What business owners should know who their customers are and how they want to be served is essential to the success of any company. Questions and surveys on social media platforms can help business owners access this information quickly. Marketing Director of Lab 5702, Social Media Strategist and Jason Burton, and, a Kansas City-based boutique marketing services agency, says that information like that can help you spot your brand in wider groups outside your original contact base. "Put your product in front of trendsetters or next user level," he says. "Specific searches enable you to dig below the ground to find supporters and possible influencers to use or support your product or service." Social service of mapping based on locations like Google Maps, Foursquare, Facebook Places, and MyTown give consumers to take advantage of their influence. You get $2 off your purchase, for example, if you visit Tucson's favorite florist and tweet it to your supporters. The network and effect, the greater the discount. The services also allow users to find events and friends and to updates, share locations, photos, comments and tips. More than 5 million users each boast Google Maps and Foursquare. Mobile apps have enabled greater social media interactivity.

What should the business professionals know Carmen Hudson, CEO of Tweeta job in Seattle till 2013, do when she was a Senior Talent Acquisition Director for Yahoo and experienced the evolution in hiring practices. "Companies cultivate and market a brand that appeals to certain types of candidates and attracts them", she explains. Social media is constantly at the forefront of this strategy for businesses like Facebook, Starbucks, Apple, and Microsoft. Recruiters, for instance, will use LinkedIn to build a search flow of attributes to precisely determine the type of candidates hiring managers with minimal time and time. "We also search for how many followers you have," says Hudson. "Are you a strong network? If you are an expert, friends, and/or fans, you are strong indicators?" The Jump Start Social Media survey conducted by hiring managers shows that 66 percent of them go to LinkedIn to find potential candidates, 23 percent go to Facebook, and 16 percent go to Twitter. "Job seekers who post and update profiles are always friendly and often first get to work," says Hudson. "Recruitment officials will perform a more inclusive search because they can now reach applicants where they are playing," says Hudson. Organizations can also promote the product and the message of the business.

What to maximize social media marketing to support your brand or business?

• A blogging platform is essential, says Warren Laidler, DeLite Multimedia's webmaster, and creative director, in New York City. Blogs have a greater capacity for organic leads because their rich nature makes it easier to scan. Search engines love and rate content-driven channels above static websites. "Think your blog as a launchpad and hub for your business. Your social media efforts should lead back to your blog or web site, which should be dynamic and informative, and which should provide content and information encouraging visitors not only to return but also to distribute their content to their network." Laidler also proposes to add RSS feeds and useful links to your blog, a great way for visitors to share information that is interesting. You can, for instance, incorporate original news, retweets, or other sources of shares, responses from references, motivational quotes, and subject topics with your Twitter schedule. Two to four tweets a day are a standard formula. Positive action can also easily grow and create a buzz that goes beyond the core audience of a company. In the virtual world, customers and job seekers will control and establish patterns by convincing the network to take action or to buy a product or service. Laidler advises that you use apps like YouScan.io to calculate your impact on social media and to learn how your messages are reached.

• Choose an image for the avatar of your social media rather than a logo, advise Twitter Power's best-selling social media author, Joel Comm.

• Use images, links, contact information, RSS feeds, etc. for individualizing your brand and promoting your product.

• Choose a third-party app or service, to allow fast, simple dissemination of posts and other content across several social media sites.

• Choose a third-party application or service. You can attach plug-ins or applications into your blog's sidebar so that visitors can easily access all of your social media.

• Don't follow anyone who follows you on Twitter. All websites in social media have plug-ins or widgets that allow quick, easy updates with one click. Conduct targeted keyword searches for individuals, businesses, and other players in the industry who are important to you or want you to be a client.

• Show your know-how. If you're in business, you're already a specialist who people want to know about valuable information, Comm says. Take advantage of your strengths, ambition, skill, and personality.

CONCLUSION

Influencer Marketing is growing, and people trust in connection with it. There are many influencers who have associated and market with big brands like Adidas, Nike, etc., the same with companies that have associated and market with big influencers, and in the same way, this idea is ideal for small companies too.

Influencer marketing was one of those major issues in digital marketing. Many influencers in all sizes come up all over the place and show their skills in promoting themselves to companies, which is also a great opportunity for companies, as they trust their audience through these influencers.

It is somewhat difficult for small businesses to stand out online and make their target audiences identify them as rivals, but they can achieve their goals and promote their products and services to a wider audience with the help of a good influencer and a good marketing campaign.

Influencers of social media are available in different sizes and niches. When it comes to social media influencing, the first thing that comes to mind are those who have millions of followers and fans, that's true, we'll call them 'Celebrities', there are 'Smaller' influencers who have less than a million followers and fans. On the contrary, there are many ways to classify influencers, not only by their audience but also their contents. Therefore, it is important for small businesses to find an influencer that suits your business perfectly or that is credible and professional enough to endorse and spread the word on your business, products and services.

Influencer Marketing for small businesses involves working with people with an active audience to promote your products and services and to disseminate your brand's concept. In this way, small companies with an influencer can hit the audience of the influencer for their own advertising, while the influent offers a sign of approval to the company. People or audiences who trust your influencer can give your company the opportunity to display and try your product. This is how advertising influencers work. From here, you begin to build an intimate relationship with your influencer, the viewer, and eventually achieve those enormous sales you count on.

Please note, in order to remain strong and sustain a long relationship, you need to be more honest, as it is necessary for all types of relationships that you do not want to offend the community as trusts.